The Girl in the Box

by
Juanita H. Imhoff

RoseDog Books
PITTSBURGH, PENNSYLVANIA 15222

ISBN-10: 0-8059-9152-2
ISBN-13: 978-0-8059-9152-9
Library of Congress Control Number: 2005938017

Printed in the United States of America

First Printing

For information or to order additional books, please write:
RoseDog Books
701 Smithfield St.
Third Floor
Pittsburgh, PA 15222
U.S.A.
1-800-834-1803
Or visit our web site and on-line bookstore at www..rosedogbookstore.com

THIS ISN'T A DREAM

I'll take you back to the time when, it's a cold winter night. I was a four years old child, and my brother lay sleeping. As i lay in the bed listening to the adults who were drinking in the living room. I couldn't help but hear their voices, they were very loud.

I could hear a male's voice saying something to my mother about sex, soon after he was talking very dirty.

The words he said scared me because i had heard these words before. It made me crawl out of my bed and into one of the boxes in the next room over.It was an empty box the only thing in that room was the boxes from our last move, i went into the biggest box and got myself confortable as i could.I tried not to make a noise, i didn't want anyone to find out where i was.

I knew he was talking about me, mom called my name out. I wouldn't listen, i heard oh! she's around here somewhere. AS i listened i could hear his shoes on the floor it sounded so loud as he got closer to where i was. An hour or so later, i thought they had forgotten about me. I hadn't heard them talking for sometime by then. I was starting to fall asleep myself. Just then i heard that same niose it was his shoes as he got closer to the room i was in again. He walked back from one room to the other, whispering my name. I didn't answer him of course, but that didn't matter. He ended his searchin the room i was in. My mother had told him where i would be it was my safe place, i felt safe or had felt safe at one time. Mom made sure i wasn't no longer, i wasn't safe anywhere, not even with my own mother. Anyway i sat in the box listening to his footstep as he got closer to the box i was in. I wouldn't even move i even tried not to breathe for fear of being found. It wasn't long until i saw a light fromj the hallway as he opened up the box where i was hiding. He pulled me by the arm out of the box, leading me by the hand to the corner of that same room. He pushed me down onto the floor facing the wall, at the sametime me told me don't scream or try to run or you will go where your grandpa is, that ment to me i would die. I felt my heart bounding it felt like it was coming out of my chest. There was a brief time when i thought my mother was coming to help me how could she not hear me crying, how could she not hear, for a brief moment i thought she was coming, but she walked on by, all i could think of was has she heard? Her walking past the room was she coming to help me! she does love me! but as she walked by i though to myself, what did i do? way is this happening to me? why doesn't she love me? i could only cry harder. I didn't do anything to deserve this so i tried to think of anything other than what was happening my mom had once told me when this thing happens to you, stair at a spot on the wall or floor and think of some else it will be over soone, so i did that night.What was happening to me didn't matter to her it was only the money she thought of for me i lost everthing inside of me. I could only go to my box and cry myself to sleep after each time this happen. It has taken years of talking to turn what happened into a learning experience for myself.I had to forgive not only the men but my mother but, when this all started the age i was i couldn't tell no one i couldn't do anything about what was going on in our home. Still today i wonder was there anything i could have done to help myself. I didn't think so at the time because for my age, plus what i was told each and everytime. I would be told if you tell not one will believe you or if i tell i will be sent to live with people that will hurt me worse, i just didn't think i had any choices at that time i really didn't. I often wonder would i have been a different person if that stuff didn't happen in our home. So many thought go through a persons head when your grow up in a home filled with hate, and being scared of your own shadow, my only safe place even as a teen was in a box.

THE JUANITA IMHOFF STORY

The things i'm about to tell you are all true. It started when i was a child of the age of two. As a matter of fact my own mother was the cause of almost everything that happened to me. Now being a mother myself i can't imagine doing anything to hurt my child. They say time heals all,in this case i found that to be untrue.

After everything that has happened to me in my life, it's a wonder why i'm not crazy i was told this on many occasions. I have been to so many doctors different doctors. In every case so far they said to me. There is no way that you could have gone through these things and not be nuts. After hearing this stuff from many people that are suppose to be professionals. I have no faith that i can ever get the help i need. It seems i will never meet someone that i can trust in totally , a person who i can tell everything to, without being judged. There are only a couple of things i'm not proud of in my life, one abusing drugs.

The other i started abusing myself thinking money was worth trading myslef for,now i work on me, staying sober, being a good mother, friend and wife. I only want to help other they say no one will believe you i will! They say your not worth anything. I had to turn my thinking around after all the things told to me, i honestly started believing in those words. Someone is out there and will listen to you some people don't care but there are more of us that do care just look i'm here.

I WON'T TELL

That day started like most everyother day. My mother had friends over to drink with her and they all decided to go out to the bars. We kids were happy they had gone out, no one happier than me. I couldn't tell anybody about the stuff that had been going on while they were out while they slept. Needless to say i was very happy, it was just us kids at home. We played games we ran, we jumping on bed. I had fun it was one of those times that stick out in my memories. It wasn't a fun life with my mom not when she had men around anyway. It started to be a daily ritual on the days when mom had men over for drinks anyway. One day my mother had a party with a lot of people over. I was scared each time this would happen, i would go to the room where the boxes were at, to hide in them. This was what i started doing when mom had males over rather than running around the house. Plus i knew i didn't tell anyone where my hiding place was and i felt safer.

Hours had past since i had gone into the boxes and no one had come looking for me. This was when i thought it to be safe to come out i didn't know what was going on out in the livingroom but i could hear peoples'voices. It was my mother and a male voice mostly, that i was listening i had heard this voice before and thought it was safe to come out. My mom said "where was she hiding" speaking about me, i know this now. When she saw me standing in the doorway, she told me to go to my room and wait, but i ran into the room where i hide in the boxes. I stayed there for hours it seemed, soon i was asleep. I woke up to my mom calling my name telling me "you get out here right now" when i did she was bugged me to tell her where my hiding spot was. Finally thinking my mom was trying to play with me, i did tell her and i showed her where it was too. This would prove to be a very big mistake. Later that same night I heard that man coming into the room calling my name saying to me "come out i won't hurt you. He kept this up for sometime then he must have gotten mad because he said he would break all the boxes and i wouldn't have a hiding stop anymore. I did crawl out at that time, as i stuck my head out from the end of the box he was waiting and, pulled me out all the way. He said if you say anything i will come back and hurt you worse. Do you understand me kid he said?

This guy scared me so badly i couldn't even talk. He said did you know if i play with your tities they will grow. Now stay still he said softly, as his finger into my pant onto my bum then he slid his finger into my virgina. He tried to put his fingers in every hole on me. He said "we were going to have sex, now be a big girl" he said as he pulled my pant off of me. He put me up on his lap putting his penis on the outside of me as he then licked his fingers to make me wet.Then as he slid it into me i screamed out and he hit me so hard he had broken a tooth in my mouth. He then turned me over, bending me in such a way that when i cried out my mouth was against the matress so my screams were muffled. I don't remember much i must have been knock out but, when i came to he was gone and the blood was all over my face and between my leg.Once my mother saw this i saw her go over to him and i heard the words you owe me more money, look at the mess you made of my daughter she yeeled at him. This was when i realized my own mother was selling me.

THAT FEELING

Last night i made my bed on the floor. I crawled into it feeling so very safe. As I lay there that same old feeling came over me. That feeling i have felt so many times in the past, I was so scared i felt someone was coming for me. As i lay in the blanket i remember feeling the warmth, the way the blanket was curled up at one end, and had crawled up the wall on the other, onto the bed that had no legs the, it was on the floor. Maybe my eyes were open for fear of closing them, i thought if i shut them i would get hurt. So instead of going to sleep i lay stairing at the ceiling. I could hear movement in the other room but, i didn't dare get up to look. The fear that came across me. I will never forget i wish i could. It's like being chased until you can't catch your breathe.

All i could do at the time was try to be as silent as i could and hope i wouldn't be found. I lay on the floor hoping he would see me or hear me, I peeked out from under the blanket to see, what i saw shocked me. It was the male the was suppose to be keeping us safe, he must have seen me lifting the blanket, becaue all the sudden the blanket lifted off of me. He said "you didn't see a thing did you? i stair hoping he would go away. This wasn't to be,he hit me and kicked me so many times i lost all feeling he put a pillow over my head hoping i would have died he left but, i wasn't. When i awoke a month had gone by i wonder even today, will these feeling ever go away? will i ever be safe?

I have really never had a normal life what ever that is. While other kids my age were outside either playing or going swimming i was in cleaning our home or doing laundry, dusting things a mother should have been doing not a child.

I have always had my safe place close by, i had boxes set up in a line with holes cut though them so i could crawl in at one end and end up at the other end. Even as a teen i did the samething. I still find myself looking at boxes as they are of my old homes, they used to be my safe place,really they were the safest place i had lived in. Even today is anyone really safe? we need are safe place, there are men raping their weman, and beating on us i have learnt one thing after all of this happened i will never be the same again. If men and my mother had not put me though what had be done to me. Would i have done what i have done to myself.

I had met a female she had bean working the street, the money she came back with daily was great, so i thought to myself instead of going with her. I would go because the money the 10 or 20 minutes that all it would be and it's over but, the feelings of hating myself even more it just got stronger. That just wouldn't go away until i stopped, In the begining thought i was hurting men soon enough i figured out the only one i was hurting was myself.

At the time i was using drugs and the money came in very handly and i did want all the money i could get my hands on at the time, but for the wrong reasons.

I would either drive myself home before midnight or my ex would pick me up, the only reason he did that is because

he knew he would get money he always did. It was either this or i would get hit by him and i get all of my money taken away from him and he would go out a get high, not bring me nothing home, at all he had done this mant times in the past. When i met what is my husband now Gordon this was the changing time for m. I had wanted and tried to quit in the past i even moved away but Mitch either followed me or i ended up moving back with him. This was the past after meeting Gordon which hated drugs, he didn't even drink anymore he had stopped drinking years before i had met him. I thought this was great. The day that made my mind up for good was in 1992 when mitch and i were in bed he wanted sex i didn't, there wasn't many times in my life i have ever wanted sex because of the stuff that has happened in my past, and i had told him everything about my past life with my mother. After all we were together for thirteen years we had talked about everything. That night when we were in bed he wanted sex. I didn't but this didn't matter to him,. I just lay there looking at the ceiling preying for it to be over with. While he was doing his thing i had a flash back of the day my real father raped my sister and i. When this happened i cried out for him to stop. I saw my dads face where his face should have been, but what he said to me i knew right there if i get out of this i will never have him again as my mate. The words he said were wait a minute im about to cum, i told him as i cried that i had just seen my dads face where his face should have been. He only could say just one more minute am just about finished. That day i had made my mnd up i don't want a man for the rest of my life, in my life if this is what life is going to be like with him, not only the unwanted sex, but drugs in my life too. I had made up my mind that night i just didn't know what i was going to do. Until i met Gordon

MOMMIE DEAREST

Lets go for a walk into the past back to when i was just two years old. It doesn't seem all that far away, even today , looking back it seems like yesterday. I was the type of child that wanted nothing more than to be around her mom, but my mother had other plans for me. I recall many times when my mother couldn't get a babysitter or she just had her friends over for drinks.

On these nights i remember being so scared i would just hide somewhere, anywhere, staying in the spot i found myself being safe for that night anyway. This were almost a daily thing, the parties seemed to go on forever.

The first time it happened to me, i was a unsuspecting child of two. I could hear them, the adults parting. I didn't want to leave my mother's side, but each time i went to her side, she would just send me away out to play with my brother and sisters or just away to be out of the house. It didn't seem as if she didn't want us kids anywhere around her, and this was very true everytime we were around her she would tell us to go, it didn't matter where just, be gone she would say. One night after she had been parting with her friends i heard her talking to a man. I heard mom say, the number one hunderd dollars. I didn't know what the money was for but, i was told in the past that if i didn't do as i was told we wouldn't be eating that day. Mom would also say things like how would your brother and sisters feel, that why they couldn't eat that night was because of you what do you think they will think of you? I heard the man get up off the chair and walk down the hallway calling my name. I didn't know what was in store for me , so i called back "what" he came into the room i was in, taking me by the hand he led me to his camper. It was on the back of his truck. I didn't want to leave my mom, she stayed in the apartment i could only cry mom screamed to me to go and to listen to this man or i would be sorry when i got back home.

I did as i was told because i always did as she asked me. Just to make her happy i did it, that way maybe she would give me some of her time. This wasn't always the case. On this night was the first time mom had made me go with a man.

Once he got me to his truck he lifted me up into the back of his camper, then he got in as well. My heart started to beat so fast it felt as if it were coming out of my chest. He told me we were going to play a game, he said that i would get used to, but i shouldn't tell anybody how the game went or i could get in trouble. He took my clothing off, as he did i cried out for him to stop, which did no good at all. He covered my mouth then he ran his hands over my body, putting his fingers inside me. He touched me all over, but at two years old i didn't understand what was going on.

All i did know was i wanted it to stop. I started to cry i guess he couldn't stand the noise becuase he took me back to my mother. As we walked into the apartment mom looked down at the floor, not at me, until i ran crying into her arms.I felt as if i were hugging an ice cube. I couldn't understand what had just happened or why she wouldn't help me. I sat infrount of her crying. It took years before i found out the truth about my mother's party life. Here are a few more stories about my life while i lived with my mother and while living in foster care.

SOMEDAY, SOMBODY

I always hopes that when a person said “i’m so very sorry” i will never do that again” I hope the person meant what they had said. Especially if he said “will you please forgive me” from the bottom of my heart i won’t hurt you again. From this the very first time i can remember, things like this were said to me more than once, i have heard every story there is or ever was said to another person i’m sure.

I was told so many things just so i wouldn’t say anything about what the man had done to me. Keep in mind i was such a lonely young child. I trusted anyone for the longest time. I was a lonely kid looking for a friend. My whole life i needed someone to talk to somebody that i could tell things to. I would say to myself someday i will find somebody a person that would listen to me, without judging me over the things that had been done to me in my life. Things my mother had made me do for her in order to get money for her drinking and drug usage.

I never did find a person that i could trust, but this didn’t stop me from looking.

I looked for so long it seemed that day would never come for me, to have someone in my life, someone that i could count on. Life would give this to me one day i hoped, it seemed it never would happen until now. Now that i’m talking to you here are somethings you may or may not believe but, everything i have written here is the truth. I hope you like reading it as much as i liked getting it off of my shoulders. Today is that someday and you are that someone.

HE'S SORRY

It was early morning with the sun flooding my bedroom. I thought to myself could anything go wrong today? as i got out of my bed. This was going to be a great day. My mother's fourth husband Berry was coming to take my brother and i to speedway race track and horse riding stables. Mom never went with us or checked up on us. Just to see if the person would really be watching us or if we were up to something ,we did this sometime just to get away from her drinking and drunk friends.

This happened to be one of those days, we only wanted to go watch the horses and, my brother loved the cars also. So we would start walking very early in the morning from where ever we were living at the time. Sometimes it would take what seemed to be hours with out being able to tell time we really didn't know nor did we care.

We lived in Calder at this time it was a very far walk to get to Speedway from our house but, it was worth it. I had loved horses since the very first time i had seen one. It was my mother fourth husband Berry that had shown me a horse and taught me how to ride, i can say he was the a good stepfather for this reason, i was three years old when i could ride a horse by myself i give thanks to him for this. I would go to speed way the same place he took me the first time he taught me to ride and i did everytime i could get away, every chance i had to our home.

There was is one day that Russ and i went when we didn't tell anyone where we were going. Mom was to busy with her male friends anyway to care where we were or where we go as long as we weren't around her so we took off to speed way. Mom did know that this was the place i loved best so i was sure if she wanted us for something she would know to go there. There was a pond out near there that in a feild blanketed with tall grass and these beautiful purple flowers that rapped around the pond this was the very spot i would go to be alone. I would lay in the tall grass close my eyes and, i could smell the flowers and hear the bees and birds as they flew by me. I would pretent this was my own place, that we lived there and get up running through the field laughing, i was so full of happiness my eyes would fill with tears. After awhile i would go back to by stop by the pond and dream. One day while i lay there i could hear a voice in the distance calling my name, who could this be i thought , no one knew i was there. I started to think it must be one of my mother friends maybe she wanted us home so i stood up so he could see where i was. He said he was there to pick me up because my mom wanted me home, so i went with him, only to find out he had lied to me. It was to late i was in his truck already he pulled me closer towards him tugging on my sweat pant i was wearing. I was tring to get away from him by moving toward the door. I would have jumped if i could have but, the truck stopped as he pulled into a field, it wasn't one i had seen in the past. He said you are going to do something with me and if your good i will take you back to where your brother is, i just remember he was still at the race track waiting for me.

I didn't even know this mans name, i didn't want to either, i only wanted to go back to where my brother was waiting for me.

When this man was parked in the feild where he felt it would be safe for him he stopped. I was told to take my clothing off as he pulled his pants down. I didn't move when he asked me to do this, i was scared of this man, he seemed mean. Once he had his pants down to his ankels he grabbed me by the arms shaking me, saying don't you listen? when you r told to do something you do it he yelled. Then me pulled my sweat pant off and threw them to the floor of his truck. At first he used his fingers touching me all over my body with his rough hands, then his penis got hard and he made me touch it, telling me what to do with it. He push my face towards it, asking 'do you know how to play pretend? i said 'yes' but i didn't know what was coming next.

As he held his hard penis in his hand he said 'pretend this is a sucker for me, if you do i will drive you back to your brother knew one thing it wasn't a sucker, did i have a choice i didn't think so. I didn't do as he said so he pushed my face towards his penis the more i puched againest his hand away from his private the more harder he puched me towards it. I tried to do as he said but, i choked and got sick on him. Once this happened i guess it was turned off he slapped me calling me names like a baby, bitch and he also said something that made me think mom did send him when he said "your mom said you will do as your told and be a big girl. He got cleaned up and took me with in a block or two of where he found me.

The only thing on my mind once i was out of his truck was to get my little brother and go home to tell my mom. The surprise i got once home was that of utter shock, he was sitting at the table drinking with my mother other were there as well all drinking around the table. He was telling and my mother what happened they started laughing at the part where i got sick.

This wasn't funny to me, i was hurting inside and i felt so unwanted. I didn't ever want this to happen again i was thinking, as this man came to me touching me with his rough hands again he took me to moms' room tearing the pant off me not caring at all that he was hurting me, he pulled his own pant down to his knees. He sat me on her bed as he was on his knees he pushed himself inside me hard not caring or thinking, i was only five years old. He push his penis into me as if he didn't care or take my age into account. I cried out as he did this to me, but no one came to my cring i thought to my self my mother will come a stop him, but this didn't happen either.

Once he was done with me he pushed me to the floor and said 'that was better but it wasn't worth it' as he pulled his pants up and left the room. I was left sitting on the floor crying not loud enough that i would be heard or i would get a licken from my mother. Mom had told me that day just before this happened that if i didn't do what i was told i wouldn't get to eat nore would my brother. The day before this one i was going into other peoples' gardens steeling vegtables so we would be able to eat. The only words that came out of the mans as he was leaving was' i'm sorry' but i knew he wasn't. My mother stood there in the doorway with her hand out as she sent me to my room. I thought to myself why isn't she yelling at him? why didn't she call the police? so many thought but nothing done to help me to get away from this it didn't look like she wanted it to stop. I found out years later why, it was all for the money.

WHAT A WONDERFUL SIGHT

I can remember this one day, when mom had called our stepfather Bob come down where we had moved to in Winnipeg. This was the only time she would time him stuff like i miss you, or i still love you, all kinds of other crap, just to get him to come to where ever we were at the time so she would have a built in sitter. I hated her playing with his feeling like she did. I heard mom on the phone talking with daddy Bob, the words that were said made me think he was on his way down to see us. Once she got off the phone her words to me were 'yes' he will be here tomorrow.

I was so happy i called out to my little brother just think dads coming to stay again, maybe this time for good, mom said no way he coming to help me with you little bastards for a week or so that all. Never the less i couldn't wait until the next day, just to see him made me happy i loved him so much he was my real daddy in my heart and mind. This time when he came down to see us we were taken to this place where you could camp over. I don't recall the name of the place, but it was about one hour west of Winnipeg. I couldn't wait to get there to show daddy Bob he hadn't seen it that place as of yet but, soon he would be seeing the most beautful place i had ever seen. Although he wasn't staying for long we had a few days with him so i hope he would have fun too. He was about to meet great people plus everything was at this park/ lake and at this place my mother loved it because they had a bar out there plus kids could come in the bar until 6pm. My brother and i took our dad to show him all the stuff they have like shaffel board, pool and booze for the adults and pop for us kids plus other people camping so it isn't like your alone, unless you want to be. The day past by to quickly for me but, the night brought more beauty. We were laying on the ground as all the other adults were up drinking around the camp fire. Once it got dark enough my brother Russell, daddy Bob and i all laid down on the ground in the grass.

As we looked at the sky, the cloud were forming shapes it was like the sky was doing magic that night just for us. The first thing we saw was a man on a cross, with his hands out to each side even with his shoulders, his legs were down and it looked as if they were stuck together on top of one another. I had never seen anything like this before.I couldn't take my eyes off of the clouds they were doing magic my eyes were transfixed to the skiesas the clouds were changing shapes. It was a good thing it wasn't just us kids that saw this, we would have never been believed by the others but some of them around the fire saw the same as we were looking at too.

The shape of the cloud started to changed, the skies opened to show us another shape.

A beautiful lady in white with a flowing vail, today i know this was the virgin Mary, after she disapeared into the skies there were shapes of all kinds of animals. Then all of the sudden the sky turned a dark black. We all took off running for different places to just get to some kind of shelter. The rain came down very hard, at the same time the wind blowing so hard, it seemed scary to me at the time i hadn't ever been outside while something like this was happening it was scary but really cool. The rain pounded down on the sandy beach. The trees were being blowen on so hard they were bending as if they were breaking i could even hear the crashing and crackles but just as everything started so quickly it ended the same way. The skies opened up again, there were the stars up there as if looking down on only us, that night they were shining so brightly they were twinkling flashing some of them were falling to the earth making it look like fireworks just for us i feel into a deep sleep. While my head was full of the days events,we only had a short time with daddy Bob he was going home soon.

That was one day and night i won't ever forget, For one thing it was the only good times i had with my mom. Nothing would ever happen to me on those times because daddy Bob was there. Ever since the very first day Bob met my mother, things started changing for the better. My mother didn't or couldn't sell me to her male friends when he was around, it's not like she stopped seeing these men because she sure didn't but, i can only recall she sold me one or two more times, That next day when we all woke up our mother was gone again she pull a dirty one on daddy Bob. This wasn't the first time she had done things like this. She would act like she was missing him and he would jump on the next train or plane just to find out not a thing is different. We got to our home thinking just maybe she was so drunk last night and got a ride home. This wasn't the case, she never called or came home for days it was very close to a week. The thing is when she did daddy Bob as always greeted her at the door as if she was ok, never did he get mad for the stuff she would do it must have hurt him deeply thinking back on it now, anyway this was the day she told me to pack up she said i was going to visit my real dad in Bellingham Washington. I didn't really want to leave i was scared if i would ever see them all again, i had never been sent away like this. Then mom said "you can see your sister for a week or two then you'll be back ok" like i had a choice but off i went that very next morning it wasn't even light outside yet and here i was getting seated on a airplane. This was first time ihad been on one plus i hadn't seen my sister for a year or so by this time it was exciting for me that morning by night time i had a totally different feeling.

NEW BABY

One day after school our mom sat us down to tell us something. We never would have guess what she was about to say, she told us she was having a baby. This wasn't something we thought would ever happen because of the parting she did. I didn't think would have the time for this baby becuase she didn't spend anytime with the kids she already had.

I will have a new baby brother or sister for you kids soon she said with a sad tone in her voice.

Mom had only just met these couple but needing someone to be with us kids while she went to the hospital we didn't get a choice either. At bed time i went to my mom room to sleep on the floor by the heater. Once i was fast asleep i heard some diggig through my mother draws, i didn't want to look up with the person seeing me for fear of being hurt if the person saw me so i lay still while looking from under the covers.

I stayed in the same spot without moving until he went back out of the window the way he came in, this confused me because it was the guy that mom let stey at our home with his wife. After he got back into the house he came in the room using the door, he came in for only one reason that was for me. I opened my eyes to see him lay down beside me he didn't waist anytime either. He put his hand under the blanket putting his finger up inside of my virgina this made me yell out loud when i did his wife said "what are you doing "he said "never mind just keep watching ou the window for her mother to get home" and let me know when you hear or see anything! My mom was seen from coming from down the road so the woman called out to him letting him know she was back. I was happy when i heard these words he said 'get up and wash up' so i did . The first thing my mom did when she came in was to go to her room and put the rings she always wore away. This was when she said to me who was in my room? i told her everything how i watched him come in fromthe window and all the other things i had to say said said i here about this later i only want to know where my rings are for now. After telling her she confrounted them telling him that he was seen while he stole them. Mom didn't get the rings back that night but thoses people were told to get out.

It was a few days later when mom had to go to the hospital she said baby was coming home with here in a couple days when she came home. I for one was very happy, i knew i would have a baby to care for. On the days we knew mom was cominghome from the hospital with the baby we ran home from school.The only thing that was on my mind the whole time mom was gone was hoe i could wait to see the baby plus the man mom was married to at the time had never had his own child, he was the best man mom ever had in her life as far as us kids knew. He had never yelled, or hit us nor did he ever hurt our mother. We sure were disappionted once we got home, my mother was there in the bed, the crib was right beside her yet no baby was in there.

When i asked mom where the baby was she said nothing at first but, minutes later our new step father took us aside to explain to us kids what miscarriage ment then he was gone , he needed time to himself as well. I was so sad i would speek for days after that, i was looking forward to having someone around that would hopefully love me, that baby was it i thought. I knew i didn't want to live there anymore because with her not pregnant and our new daddy gone. I was going to be hurt again so mom could have money again. I didn't find out until years later that mother went to the hospital to have an abortion, not to have a baby. She didn't want another child in her live daddy Bob told me this and i felt so badly for him. To this day he never had his own children and my mother took the one chance he had of being a father away from him, Of any person on the planet that i know he would have been the best father.

THE NIGHTS WERE WORST

The days and nights passed slowly but, the weekends finally got there i would think to myself 'much better' because we could go out somewhere. On the weekends russ and i would do the samething every weekend just to get out of the house. To be away from mom and her friends the male ones anyway. Mostly we would go to a place called Speedway mom's third husband had taken us in the past where he taught me how to ride a horse i fell in love with the place horse were there, i have loved horses since i can remember, but this was also a race track for cars as well. This was the best place to go to for us anyway. We lived in the North end of Edmonton, the Speedway was there too it was a couple hours if we walked. On days we had gotten money from mom's male friends we would took the bus. This way we got there alot faster. Anyway mom didn't care where we were sometimes i felt she wish we weren't even born. I found out she only had us around for the extra money that came in monthly from the government. We kis just had to come up with way to stay out of her way, by thinking ofstuff to do. As long as it wasn't raining i knew exactly what i wanted to do.

I didn't want to be there either, i wanted to sleep out with the horses i knew i would be happier and safer. Not once did our mom ask us where we were going or any of the questions a good parent would or should have asked.

All this time i thought i had a real family. It wasn't until years later when i saw how other families act around each other in and out of thier homes, they were nothing like we are, i would think to myself, how badly i wish i could have a mother and father that loved me. How great would it be to say to my friends my mom and dad took us camping last weekend or anything really i would have given anything for this kind of family. I was stuck with family the i was given, i know i 'am here on earth for a reason what this is i don't know but, i do know i'am here until GOD takes me because. i tried many times to take my own life, it never work out i'am still here. There was one good think out of being around my mother that being when my mother getting married to her fourth husband Bob Loblick he was the best man, i had ever met a man that loved us kid. My mother would have a live in baby sitter now we wouldn't be left alone or with drunk that were only there to hurt me now mom would have herself a built in baby sitter, i thought to myself. After this wedding i wouldn't be hurt no longer by these men. I sure was happy about this happening soon. i only had a few weeks to get through now. He was the first dad that would come outside with us and play, he never ever got bad at anyone. I have seen him drunk in the pasted but, i have never seen him fight, argue or hit anyone male or famale.

The sad thing was mom wanted a divorce again, just like all her other marrages they would only last for a short time. Her longest one was just under one year that was to my father, the shortest one was three weeks. when she married Berry B after getting married in the Cromdale hotel a person couldn't expect much of a start. My mother told me the day they were married she went home with the best man, and Berry with the maid of honor they weren't off to a very good start. I could only cry knowing i would not have my saftey net around no longer, when she wanted nothing to do with daddy Bob. He

was different from all the other he didn't leave us he did as mom asked but, they stayed married still for 25 years, they just didn't live together he went back to live with his mom. It wouldn't be the end of seeing him, he was around almost everyday

i thank the Lord for this i was save most days but, mom got back into her same old thing of selling me when he wasn't coming over i think she had made plans before hand so he didn't find out what she really was doing to me. After sometime had past i think he knew something was going on with me because he would come over just to take me driving around all

day and at night time some night he would pass out at our place so nothing happened to me like i said until one day she said moving day. I thought to myself oh no here we go again.

HERE HE COMES

I had been back living with my mother for two week at the time, it was in the spring of 1969. My mother lived in Calder an area on the east side of Edmonton. She told me that the baby sitter was on the way as she went to bingo. I had a very bad feeling when she told me this was a male sitter that was the way over, i cried and begged her not to go, but nothing worked she only saw what she wanted to see.

Even when he arrived i cried out that he was going to hurt me. They both laughed at what i had said, but I sure wasn't. I started getting these feelings it happened so often i just knew when it was about to happenagain.Nothing was going to stop her from going out it never did in the past why should it now. As she left out the door i told her i would be hurt by him so i was going to hide from him until she got back, she said 'don't you dare hide on him he will worry about where you are, he won't hurt you 'she let out a giggled as she walked out the door. Once mom was gone it only took a few minutes for him to feel comfortable, he said to me do you want to play a game as he sat in a chair in the living room, i just looked at him i didn't know if he ment the kind of games those othe rguys had played with me i sure didn't want this to happen again. He again said well do you want to play a game with me i didn't want to but, i thought this was a real game so i walked very slowly towards the chair where he sat. I saw his hand come out and as sson as i did i turned and ran, i don't know just how far i got before he was infount of me. I told him i have to go to the bathroom i tought i couldget away and hide if he let me go that would be the only chance i would have to get away from him. That was just what i tried to do once i got into the bathroom i jumped out the window down into the grass below and ran. I only made it to the corner when i felt a hand on my shoulders and back.

I ended up back at my house with this man at first it wasn't so bad but, that didn't last long he soon started talking about that game again. He said it was a game only kids can play, i told him i didn't want to play over and over i never wanted to play that game again it hurts i said. It didn't matter why he even asked me it wasn't like i had a chioce. He ask me to sit on his lap as i did he took my hand making me touch his penis rubbing it using my hand. I pulled it away at the same time he pull me toward his penis even harder. I knew what was about to happen i was sure it was the same things that the other men had done to me and it was happening again. He got up taking me by the hand, leading me to my bedroom. He laid down pulling me on top of him, i screamed and tried to run but, he was a little faster than i was. This man was very mean, he was fast too. I went torun but, he hit my throat so hard that i can't scream, even to this day. He laid pulling my hand towards his penis again, making me rub him, now he pulled it out of his pants i remember the smell and i had never seen this up close before. With the light on it. I was very scared of what it or he would do, i was still crying as he made me wrap my hand around his penis, and move my hand up and down along the shaft of this thing. I could tell that he was getting upset with me. His face went red slapped me again and again. I tried to scream again, only to find out i still had no voice, this from hit in my throat. He tied me up and this is where i stayed until my mother arrived back home. Before he left he said as he pointed his finger at me saying "i will come back to play that game again if you tell, if you say anything to anyone remember. Even at the time at that age i remember thinking i would never do this to my children i would listen to him, to this day i will listen to a child before believe in an adult, still to this day, my safe place still isn't around people. It is while i am on my horses back.

ALL I EVER WANTED

I was always the good kid, i tried to please my mother at all times. If she said she wanted something i was the first one to jumped for her.I would do anything for the love of my mother. I thought one day that she went a little to far. What did i know i was only four years old at the time. Plus i had already been a good girl for her many times in the past if you know what i mean.

My mom went on to tell me all i had to do was lay on the bed and not to cry to let this man do what he wanted to do to me, she said just look at the ceiling or wall and think of something other than what he was doing to me, she said will you be a good girl for your mommie said said. Me being to good one i said 'yes mommie'.

At such a young age for one thing i didn't understand how this would effect me when i grew up. Another thing is i only wanted my mom to love me plus she said i can have good food after this man going home. The only food we ever had in our place is beans or macaroni and cheese so i thought i was getting something different other than this. My didn't tell how how badly i would feel as his fingers touched me even though she had said things to me befor ehand i didn't really understand what she was saying to me. All i knew or thought was at that time my mom loved me for being good she talked to me in a nice voice and touched me she didn't hug me or kiss me i don't remember ever getting effection from her really until my after my son was born.

I did hear that day i will love you more if you do this for me, so i did. There were so many times. I couldn't count nor remember when she made me do something i didn't want to do. It was all for her so she had money. Most times she would ask 'do you want to eat today? most times we would still get the same old thing beans or macand cheese. On the other hand mom always had money to drink or go out to get drunk just about everyday. There were many days i remember going to bed hungry until one day we learnt a trick by some one i don't recall who, but it was raping bread into a cloth with sugar in it then you suck on it it helped as i remember. I thought things like this only happened in the thrid world countries, but it's here as well. My mother made sure she had what she wanted. Us kids on the other hand were just an imposition. I was the only girl around since i was three because my older sisters were taken by the fathers. I didn't understand why i wasn't taken too at the time i thought it was that my father din't care. My sister told me years later that mom was making money selling me so this was why would she wouldn't let me go. After my older sister had gone it was a big change it was my brother and i both hiding we only came out for food if there was any when we did come out we displayed caution. We were scared of our mother friends the males ones anyway. Some of these guys would get us to smoke cigars and make us sick while they just laughed or they would feed us booze. They thought this was funny too. One night mom didn't have a sitter for my brother and i she told me to follow her outside,It was wintersoi put on my boots and a coat i never had my own so i took what was there. I thought we were going somewhere as we walked i thought we were going to her friends we called auntie Rose which was living upstairs at the time.

We were almost to the top of the stairs when she along with her male friends started to laugh, when mom said stick your toung to this, with them laughing i didn't think anything bad would happen to me plus i wanted to make my momie happy by being a good girl so i did as i was asked. My toung was stuck to this steel rail "i guess she got her babysitter"i don't recall how much time past. What i do remember is that auntie Rose came down the stairs she poured warm water onto my toung to get me off the steel, once i was off it was bleeding and i couldn't speak well for a few days after. I don't know what if anything was said to my mother about this. I do know that i heard auntie Rose saying to someone on the phone that she didn't think my mom would go this far. I thought to myself at the time if you only knew what she does to me.

That night i tried to tell her somethings that were going on like what the men were doing to me, when she cut me off and asked where is your mom when this is goingon? i told her right there most times. She didn't believe me, it was hard to listen to that for sure. After asking for help from the one person i trusted. When she didn't think i was being honest how would anyone else believe what was going on was my thinking . After all i was just a kid, i had been told this many times your just a kid or you nust have asked for it so i learnt to keep my mouth shut. Mom would say you think you have it badly here at home i will send you where peole are that don't love and you will see what being hurt is. After tell Rose when she didn't believe me or help me, i kept it to myself,i was to afraid to say anything again i was dammed no matter what i did.

THE FOSTER HOMES

My brother and i had just arrived back to Edmonton from living in the USA with our real father Jim and his new wife Jan. I was so happy as soon as my eyes met with my Grandfathers after all he was the one that paid the plane tickets that got me home. My momther was there as well as a few aunts they showed up because of the reason i was sent back to Edmonton, they wanted to know what really happened from my mouth. Once we were all into the car i started by cring i was asked by my grandpa what happened to you kids down there? I told them how much we hated it and being so excited about finally being back i just rambled on. They wouldn't let my sister Theresa come back, mom asked why i told them 'this morning when we found out we were coming home dad said as he held the tickets in his hand who wants to go back to their mother Russel said i do, my sister said i want to go too, i yelled happily i want to go, just then Jan his wife said you can't let both girls go who will do the cleaning i'am not doing it. They told my sister said wasn't going back with us, i remember how hard she cried when she was told this. After all she had been with them longer than i had been and from day one of being there it was like being a slave to them. We did all the cooking,cleaning, laundry all so, if we didn't keep our grades up to what they wanted them to be even if we were doing our best, we were beat for this as well as every other reason they could think of. My first beating down there was because i got gum for all of us i had welts and blisters after that first time. Iwas telling them all of this stuff and i heard in the back seat what happened last night? I told them how it was Jans' birthday we all went to a lake, this was where they got drunk and started to fight. Jan took off and Jim couldn't talk her back into the car. We went home without her once we got home dad sent us to bed it was still light outside but this wasn't anything new we had been sent to bed many, many time in the past while we were with them for reasons like Jan would run her finger on a table and if she could find a piece of lint on anything and believe me she look for it, she hated us she would do anything to find a reason to hit us. They said it couldn't be that bad, as i started to saying i knew you wouldn't believe us.

I went on to say none of this stuff happened to the bot or to her kids just Theresa and i and Russ could tell you this too. Last night i went on to say was bad dad came into our room when it was dark out and hurt us girls. They wanted to know exactly howso i told them. He came in the room Theresa and i had traded places in the bed i was facing her and she was faced towards the door when dad came in, he walked over to the bed laing down he picked her up making her face that this he pees from and made her choke on it, when Theresa threw up he turned her over and put his thing inside her when he was done she had blood on her and the bed all over, so he said go clean up, but first wake your sister to send her into my room. I had seen everything he did to her i didn't want this to happen to me so i pretended i was sleeping, she told him that she couldn't wake me, that when he said i'll get her up. He came back into our room grabbing me by the hair and dragging me intohis room closing the door behind him.

He picked me up putting me on his bed he took off his robe and telling me off with the cloths at the same time. I was very scared of him i always was i knew how mean he was, so i did as i was told he got on top of me as he was working his penis into my virgina i noticed the phone beside his bed it was one of those old fashion ones, i picked it up it was so heavy that when i hit him on the head with it mostly it just fell out of my hand onto his head. It seemed to knock him out when he didn't move or say anything so i squirmed from under him and ran to my sister in the bathroom tell her we should run to Jans' parents place for help. We knew they didn't like us either they only liked their grandchildern but what choice did we have we ran, they lived in the same trailor park as we were in just across the road. We got to their dorr out of breathe and scared thinking dad may have gotten up and after us, Theresa got the words out through the tears what had happened all they said was go to bed we take care of this, it seemed they were mad at us. When we got up this morning that when we we told everything and now here i am but Theresa couldn't come. Grandpa said he was going to charge my dad and he did. I was questioned many time and my sister was i on the other end. Life when on while being back with my mother she still was having her parties and still all kind of men coming and going she evn sold me twice but someone saw that didn't like what mom had done and told on her while mom was being investigated she had some friends come to visit from out of town. We knew their son from before his name was Loyd, littlwe did i know when this day began this would be the last day with my mother all thanks to my brother he and i didn't get along that great. He always wanted mom to himself and would fight with me all of the time to get his way and he always did. My mother sided with him on everything. The parent went out for drinks while loyd was playing over with us, we wanted to play making phank phone calls. The thing was only Russell got to make the calls, when loyd said 'it's my turn ' my brother said ' you want a turn, have one" as he hit him in the head split opened. The police were called in and things moved so fast from there, all i knew is we went to our first foster home that day we woke up in the children centre the next morning. That was the start of a whole new thing for me. When it came to court in the States was i was to young to testify. I thought they would come back with my sister Theresa but, they didn't. I only heard about things that went on when i got to use the phone, because i was in a place that you can only see your family if they come to see you, and my mother didin't take the time to do anything like that not for me anyway. We went on from there to a nothing place called Marydale on the southside of Edmonton. Then we went to a foster home in Smokey lake all in summer of 1971. By that fall the people we were living with in Smokey Lake were sick of my brother, he was doing all kinds of bad stuff. One day, he let one of the milk cows into a field of alphalpa killing her within hours he just laughed, one sunday the female pig was having her litter and i have always love all animals. So i asked if i could stay home from church that day, i wanted to be ther if the mother pig needed help with her pigelts as they came out i would help the mother. I thought i was doing a good thing i liked learning about this sort of thing anyway. When they came home that day, and saw me in with the mother pig helping her clean them they must have thought i was doing a good thing. They gave me the runt. My brother was mad he didn't like when i got anything or if someone paid any kind of attention to me, he would do something to hurt me. He had always been the attention getter so killed my baby pig by drowning her. He has been like this for as long as i have been around my brother. He would lie saying i did something i didn't do or say anything to get me into trouble. Mean while he was doing all the bad stuff like starting fires and much this like stealing, fighting anything and everything. He always said that i did what ever it was he had done and with my mom would believe him everytime. These people knew i wouldn't do anything to an animal, plus my Russell was fighting with their kids all the time. Where i was concerned i was a good kid they had told my social worker this too i heard them talking one day just before we left there. Their daughter and i were talking about the things my borther does to me. They must have heard what we were talking about the next time we moved it was to different places. It was that next week when they told me welfare had found me a home one where i could stay until i grew up. If i'am good like i' am around them i wouldn't be moving around no more plus, it was on a farm i was moving to. I couldn't have been happier i started to think, i will have my own horse, maybe they have animals all sorts of thought crossed my mind. They had to ask my new foster family if they could give me the black kitten i had at their place and they said yes, so i got to bring her with me i was alone.

TOMAHAWK FOSTER HOME

It was September 1971, when i first walked into the Zanders home. I was told that Charlie and Hilda that i could call them dad and mom if i wanted to, and me being the kid i was i only wanted to please adults so this is what i called them. I had a weekend to get used to being there, before going to school on that following Monday. On the first Sunday we went to church and from that first weekend i only missed one day of going to church. It didn't take me long to get into the hang of things out there i didn't have to do much at first they were very nice i helped with house work doing dishes sometimes. Outside on the other hand was a different story. Hilda being in her fifties and Charlie sixty two years old when i first move in with them, they couldn't do that much. I wanted to help anyway to make them happy to show i'am a good girl so i did more than i was asked to do for them.

They only had a wood stove for cooking and most of the heat came from the stove so i had to chop wood everyday to make sure we didn't run out. On Sunday we would butcher a few chicken and in the summer time i would help her in her garden. The best part of hanging around Charlie was he would go to the river to fish it only being two miles down the road he would take me with him once or twice a week. The other thing he did for a hobby was buying old cars he would fixed them up for resale and every fall he went hunting. I didn't like this because i loved animals so i just wouldn't eat much meat, and i still don't. Hilda was always going to something to do with the church, like ladies aid, bible study group and what ever there was going on in the church she was there. I got myself into confermation and the youth group they were both very please to hear i wanted to do this without them asking me to do any of it.

So the first year of living with them i had made sure i was doing something everyday it all had to do with the church as well. Plus in that first year i had learnt to change oil in the old cars for him. I couldn't ever stop talking about having my own horse from the first day we met so they had told me if i was there next year i could get my very own pony. The dael we made was i would have to work to buy feed for my own horse. It was the summer of 1972 when they had told me i was getting my family allowance this surprised me plus they told me we were going to pick me out my own pony that weekend. I couldn't have been happier the day couldn't come fast enough for me. The day did go and go now i had to buy feed for him. I had named my horse lightening. My life was great for those first two years but it was about to change in a way i was not going to like at all. It was after church on a Sunday afternoon when my foster parent cousen came over for a visit. I foundout later it was planned forhim to come over because he was giving me the job i needed to buy the feed for my horse. It was good for awhile but i was learning nothing good lasts not for me anyway. At first i would go to his place on either Saturday or after church on Sunday my job was to clean his trailor for him and sometimes he needed help with feeding his cows. He had over two hundred of them and i didn't mind the work at all. It was the animals i wanted to be around anyway but he was nice at first. Each week he would ask me if i wanted any treats for the next weekend that i was to come over. I thought this guy is so nice but after a month or two he said "your nails are dirty come over here i will clean them for you"so i did i sure didn't think he was going to do anything to me. At first he did my nail but he soon said to me i can't reach them very well but if you were to sit on my lap i could do a better job. I had sat on a man lap before and it wasn't nice I ended up getting with this man raping me. This was when i told him i didn't need them done i would do clean them in the bath later. He didn't take no for an answer he said he wasn't going to hurt me and the way he was being so nice to me i thought he wasn't going to hurt me. I also thought if i didn't listen to him i wouldn't have the job and they would make me sell my lightening my horse. They had told me when i first got him they said you pay for the feed for your own horse and you can keep him. I took this very seriously i didn't want to loose him either so i moved over onto his lap. This was the firdt day he started touching me in places that made me feel very uncomfortable. As i said all i could keep thinking aboutis lightening and having to move again so i kept goingover to his place every weekend. I tried to talk with my pastor since i was with him each day for some amount of time most tims other were around him too i wasn't sure if i could tell him. These questions kept running throught my mind. I wondered will he believe me? will he tell my foster parent? Will he get uncle bill put in jail? this is what would scare me. I didn't want to move or leave my horse plus no one ever helped me in the past so i said nothing. Besides i didn't know he was doing anything wrong. It had been my experience that men are aloud to do as they pleased to little girls like me, it was done to me so many times with nothing happening to the male that had hurt in the past. I really didn't know what to do until on day i just had enough.

It was June 13 1979 school was just about out for the summer I had been through so much i only wanted it all to stop. While going to that School because of being a foster child i had been teased almost daily. The girls had put tampons in the locker or dirty panties mean stuff like this so that i would be made fun of and teased. After school i couldn't wait to get finished at church because i knew after this i would be with lightening. He was my best friend he followed me around like a dog the only other animals i ever had was my cat but he had since past away and my calf. One Sunday i had been sick like i said i only missed one day of church this was the one day. It was because of the old cow named ma was having her calf and i wanted to be there just incase so they let me stay home that day. By the time they got home they came to the barn to see what i was doing with my horse in there. They stopped as they got to the barn just to watched me. What i had done, when i saw the yellow of the calves feet, i knew it was backwards so i got a rope and tied it to lightening neck he and i were so close when i told him back he did just that he took a few steps back and helped me pull the calf out. Once the calf was cleaned up and doing good Hilda told me the calf was mine, so now i had to think of him too. I had trained him so i could ride him and lightening would follow me we did this is the parades and in the opening of the rodeo's i was known for being a good trainer. Until one day Charlie and Hilda told me i could go riding my horse down the road this is something i had never been aloud to do so i thought they were just trusting me eoungh to go and be safe while riding on the road. I wasn't that far when i heard a gum shot, i turned him back towards home but, by the time i got there my calf aticua was dead he was hanging up side down with his guts on the ground i ran off cring.

Now i had lots to think about after all really i paid for my own horse and i paid for all the feed for 7 years not only for my horse but their cows too. It was my hey that fed them as well, not that i minded at the time, but now i wanted to leave with lightening. All i could think of is who can i talk to? again these thoughts going through my head. Like i said it was June 13 when i lost it. I wouldn't listen in school i had a problem with this teacher for years. He had picking on me, teased me just for being in foster care. He wasn't the only one and after all the years of this going on plus the lies and being called names and all the threats. I had this happening to me so many time in those years. I was told if i didn't do as i was told i would be sent away from my horse and uncle Bill told me 'i hope your not thinking of telling anyone because if you do no body will listen, no one will believe you "your just a foster child your own mother didn't want youfrom being such a kind guy to this person that was the same as all the other men. I had been threatened with everything i loved the most i had to have it stop. That day in school when that teacher said when i wasn't listening like i did in the past. He could have asked me if i wanted to talk instead he said "i can see how someone like you could act out after all your mother is a slut right? he said. When he finished saying those words i hit him with his yard stick i broke it over his head. Then ran out of the school my best friend Melody had heard what happened and she was one person that didn't really do as much as all the other girls she did follow the popular girl when they put tampons in the locker i was using she was involved with that but she was the one i was closet to she went to chruch, youth group and we both were inconfermation for three years together. We did get close and when she saw me running from the school after hearing what happened she was the one to call our pastor R Mayon. Next thing i knew was he pulled up beside me as i was walking toward the town of Tomahawk. I don't know where i was going or what i was going to do i was just going, when he had his window down and called to me in that comforting voice he had he asked me "do you want to get some off of your mind and lighten your heart? I broke down i cried harder than i have ever cried in the past i couldn't help it. He took me to his place to talk it was beside the church i was still tearful by the time we got to his place. He knew something had been happening to me he said he could tell something had been wrong for some time now but it wasn't his place unless he knew for a fact. Once i opened up to him i couldn't stop i wanted to let it all out, but on the other hand i fearful of what would become of me once i did tell all. I started to talk then went on for at least 3 hours.

The thing i remember is he never stopped me once nor when i was done did he say i don't believe you. I didn't know what was going to happen but my foster parents weren't innocent in this. Charlie had been touching my tits it was the second time in my life i had heard a male say if i play with them they will grow. After i stopped talking with pastor Mayon he left the room i didn't know what was going to come next for me. The pastor did tell me nothing bad will happen to you trust me. He said you didn't do anything wrong it was them taking advantage of you then he was gone to do what ever it was that was going to take place next.

Only a few minutes had pasted when me walked back into the room, he told me i was able to stay at Melody"s place for a couple of days while welfare figures out if my mother has changed enough to take me back home with her. Turns out i got to go home with my mom. It was that first night at home with her when i knew nothing had changed.

SHE'S GONE

After all i had been though being a daughter to my mother, it was about to hurt more than i had ever thought possible.

We had been told that mom had cancer a couple of years ago but it had been in remission for around one year. I now had to move to Olds Alberta. I was starting Collage to be a vet since i loved animals as i do. I was only a few months that i had been involved in my classes my son and i were very happy living there. I went to school in the day time and worked nights in a bar so i could pay for the horse i had just gotten for my son and i. It was hard going to school and being a mom i couldn't spend the time i wanted to with him so i started picking him up for lunches and when i had homework hour. I would pick him up so we could go to this pond my boyfriend Chris would take us to when we went fishing. This was a small pond with a deck to sit on. It was great Mitchell could run around playing, while i did my homework plus we got to spend time together.

It was December 21,1990 when i recieved a call at the school from my mother. The she said that her skin cancer had come back and it was moving very fast thoughout her body. She had been moved into the palitive care unit in the cancer clinic.

I told her i would pack my things and be there that nightI will be the one to care for her. I didn't want her staying in a hospital waiting to past on. I told her i was going to find a place for her, Mitchell my son, and myself. I hung up the phone ran out of the school not taking a thing with me. I went home just taking my sons stuff and my clothing i left everything else behind.

This would be the time to talk with her and find out the things i had wanted to know as a child get these questions answered and maybe have a mother daughter relationship before she is gone.

The next day i many places to go see because that next day my mother was getting out of the hospital. It didn't take me long to find the place pack her old place up and have our new place all unpacked and looking like a home. My dady Bob had gone to the hospital to pick her up, they had been such good friends for years, he was the man i consided my father too. Thoughout everything he stuck beside mom and he had always been there for me as well this was going to be hard on him the look in his face said it all. Anyway he was helping her to our new place plus he wanted to see it. He couldn't believe what he saw when they walked in. I had supper cooking, you could hear my son was playing and it looked lived in. Everything was as if we had been there for months she was happy , i had made daddy Bob happy too by doing this for her. I had my reasons for it as well besides i loved her she was my mother. It all worked out good for eighteen months we got along great, mom seemed to fight harder for her life because of my son being around her she would give up. This was a good thing everyone was telling me. The health nurses had been telling me for months to take some time for myself, but i didn't want to leave my mother. Plus my moms' sister was starting to hang around and i had be having problems with her for years. I didn't like her much anymore she always started fights between us, she would cause some sort of trouble she always did. If i were to take a day off away from my mother i worry if she would be there when i got back. My mother sister Darleen was up to something everytime she was over i would hear her tring to talk my mom into moving in with her. Darleen was tellingher lies like one of the were she told my mom that i had called her askinh her to take my momer i didn't want to care for her anymore, which was a lie. My mom did tell me what she said but all the medication mom was on she didn't remember stuff we had talked about the day before so this worried me. One day i had called a friend of my mom that i had known since i was small her name was Rose i loved her and trusted her more than Darleen anyday, i asked her if she would come to spend the night, we had made plans or so i thought she was to be at our place the next day around 2pm so i went accross the road to my son's fathers'place for the night. I missed my mom and wondered all night how she was so i got up at 7am and went home. I opened the door to see that all my fears were confermed. Darleen had called Rose to say she would be the care giver and they all ready had the plan in place she move my mother to her place. My mother and i had made all the funeral plans, she had picked her plot and the casket. We had gone to take care of all of this months ago. When my mother left i was hurt, sad and i had a mountain of feelings of hate for Darleen. I had never had feeling likes this, not this strong anyway. After Darleen had moved my mother to her place it only took two and a half weeks for me to get the call the my mother was back in the hospital. My mother now was doing very badly, i went to see her and she was no longer the same. My mother had lost so much weight and she wasn't fighting for life the way she was when we were living together. My son had lots to doing with my mother fighting for her life at the time of her sickness. Melody and i had taken my son out halloweening then Mitchell went to his grandparent places to go out again. I stayed home i had decided to call my sister Theresa in the States to tell her how our mom was. This was the night i found out somethings the bugged me badly. I had just told me sister our mom is dieing when she said "your mom you mean" i said how is it that our real dad can rape both of us and you stay with him all these years , he either beat you into saying nothing or paid you off to shut up" she said "well maybe but your mother sold you for money for her drugs and drinking how do you think she was having all those nights out. This was the point where i hung the phone up. I couldn't wait for the rest of my answers no longer i went back to the hospital. As soon as i walk into the room where my mother was she knew something was up. I said we have to talk now mom, i went on to say i thought while we were living together you told me everything so you could go to the Lord with a clear sole. I yelled out you did do thid did you? I told her about trhe conversation my sister and i just had as i was telling her the story i could see her eyes fill with tears. I sat saying nothing for a minute because i was so hurt after all i had done for her once again i was the one being thrown away i should have been used to it but, i thought in my heart she had done some changing. I cried out "way can't you tell me the truth for once don't i deserve this much" She cried as she said how could i tell you the only one that has helped me though this thing never missing a doctors visit, quiting collage to take care of me Juanita how could i tell you i sold you to those men i 'am so sorry. She broke down cring hard as once again i took her by the hand knowinh she was so close to leaving us i said "now don't you feel better for getting this off you chest? she moving her head up and down as if to say yes but still in tears. I said mom i have time to work on what happened to me in my life you don't have the time i do please let me know if there is anymore. There wasn't i figure was she did to only me was enough, she told me my sister were not sold because of their age they were two years older than i plus they didn't listen like i did either. My mother knew i was the perfect patsy for her to use.

I left that night and as it turned out it would be the last time i saw her alive. I just couldn't go back for one month and when that day came my brother was suposed to pick me up at 2pm. As normal he did thing at his own time he kept calling and me changing the time. It was 7pm when my phone rang, i looked at the call display it was the General hospital number. I remember thinking mom never called me before as i picked the phone up putting it to my ear. The voice on the other end said "i'am sorry to be the barer of bad new, but your mother has taken a turn for the worse. I yelled out i'm on my way she said i so sorry she is gone she past just now at 7:02pm. I got mad because i had been calling the hospital all day asking how my mom was doing i made at least ten call that day to the hospital not one time was i told of the changes in my mother health when i asked why this was she told me your aunt Darleen said you didn't need to watch this. I never did forgive Darleen for this or the what she did after my past away. I never knew my mother gave her the bank card. I didn't know who was taking care of paying for the funeral or if it had been done because daddy Bob was up to see her everyday i thought maybe he was taking care of it but Darleen had talked her out of this too. Once mom was gone everything had been changed by Darleen all that mom and i had done was for nothing our arrangments of her funeral were no more Darleen called me to say she was using the limo and i could walk over there with my friends, she then said i don't know what your doing after the funeral but, we are all coming to my place but there isn't room for you and your friends i just hung up the phone that was the very last time i talked to her.

The wake took place on December 3,1992. I lived just across to road from Westlawn memoral so we dicided to walk over i had never been to a wake and i had gone to sit at the bus stop just in frount of Westlawn when daddy Bob,Mitchell my sons'dad and Melody my best friend showed up. We all walked in togetheras we went into the place daddy Bob walked in a room to the back and on the left hand side, melody went in the same room following dad, but she turned to the right where pictures were on the wall i walked in and hit the floor as soon as i saw awoman in a casket in the corner of the room. I walked over slowly looking at this person as i lost it i cried harder than i have ever cried in my live. At the same time i was saking way is this woman in here? i heard a voice say that is your mother. I had a ring in my hand and a letter to give my mother that i wanted her to take with herbut, i just couldn't believe this was her she didn't look like my mom they took her glasses and her rings necklace everything was gone it just wasn't my mom to me. I fell to my knees crying and put the ring and letter in her cold hands and i heard someone say you should take her to the hospital she need some help. I got up and ran out, i was told months later that everyone was there standing behind me. The thing is i didn't see anyone around i thought we were alone. The nexr day was the funeral this was the last straw for Darleen. They pulled up in the limo, Melody h daddy Bob and i were in the family room after all we were her family. Darleen came over saying to Melody this rrom is for family only. I turned looking at the witch as i said "if anyone is family Mel is" her and mom lived together for years as well as she has been in our family since i was seven years old, 'you on the other hand have two people in this room that i don't even know nor did my mother" Melody said i'll just go! i said this isn't my family Mel you are as i got up and left with her. We went into the room where everyone else was seated. After the service we walked following the funeral car to where my mom would be resting forever it sure didn't look like the place we had pick for her. At the hole in the ground is where the pastor said his preyer and a speech, he knew me because of the times he had come over. When my mother was still alive and her and i made all of the arrangements so why is he standing over there giving them flowers i thought to myself as i started to cry again. Daddy Bob had made me promise as did my mother in the past that i wouldn't beat her up at the funeral, daddy Bon took my hand holding it tightly. He knew i wanted to jump over the grave and grab Darleen by her neck. Just then a few people that knew want i had done, back when i quit collage to take care of my mom and i did by myself for 18 months.

They took the whole ring of flowers and walked over to me saying Juanita if anyone deserves these you do, no one has stoped their lives as you have for your mom i know she is looking down on us and isn't very happy with today. I said knowing my mother wanted me to be good once more. I told them thank you as i cried. Everyone all except Darleen had told me later on in year that i did the right thing while Darleen wrecked everything. When i found out i was sick i went to that same funeral home because my mother and i had it made so i could be put on top of her this was when i found out Darleen had yet again changed thing my mother was in a welfare hole so i couldn't be with her at my time of death. I went on to find out she had my mother bank card and got herself a car i guess when you take care of a family member for two weeks you get a car. Well i now was thinking how is my mom going to get her head stone, so i went and found one i could afford, Darleen found out and my grandma called me to say "please don't put yours on? i have one on the train right now your mom will have a head stone"so i got my money back. This is part of the reason i writting this book now, my mother still doesn't have a head stone to this day.

ONE NIGHT

It was a warm winter night i sat at home alone, it was just after my mom had past away.I was very down about everything.Just about this time the phone rang, it was a girl i had met the month before. She wanted to meet up with meet up to do some cocaine. I went, what a mistake at would turn out to be. I should have thought about it first. I should have ran out thr door but at the time i wasn't thinking. I could only see the pain in my heart from the loss of my mom. When we ran out of the drugs she asked me to come with her as she worked the street she was a hooker she said i would get paid for taking plates on the cars if i helped her i went.This wasn't whereit ended i saw how much money was in what she did. They came a day when one guy said he didn't want her but he wouldgive me twoo hunderd for a few munites of my time i thought about how much dope i could get not about anything else and off i went with him. At first i thought back to what my momused to say to me and it worded i would think about anything other than what i was doing. I would think that i' am hurting the male nothing wrong with me i wasn't thinking about anything but, the drugs.

I would stay on drugs each and everyday, until i went to jail the first time, and at the time i had to get straight. At this time i started to think about what i was doing to myself to my life and my sons' life, all because of my drug problems. At the time when i went into jail was when i started to look at what my life had been and what i had turned it into. It had to stop.I had to start dealing with the rapes and with what my mother had done to me as a child this was the hardest thing i had ever done i was not on drugs and facing the truth at times the pain was so bad i tried to kill myself in a couple different ways pills one time and cutting my wrist on another. Each time i lived this was when i had to thinking like i said in the past maybe there is a reason for why all this has happened to me. After all i had been through i can't figure out and i have no excuse for what i have done in my life all i can say is i couldn't face my mother death and for a time i was easier to be on drugs, i just could live my life staying on these drugs. I was given a death sentence from my sons' father when i was saying how he would come home with craps and be cheating this wasn't all he had done to me. We started to us needles and when we used them i had a place for mine while his were in a different place one monring he took my needle and used it knowing full well he had been out cheating and sharing needles with other girls. He didn't bother telling me or throwing it away he knew i would have never used anyones' needle ever he knew me. I had a knnock at the door on day it was a lady that worked for a health clinic in the west end of Edmonton. She told my son father had been cheating on me and one other girl had contracted hepititisi. I had to go with her and take my son so he could get the shots to make sure he wouldn't get sick. For me it was to late i had it and because of using the drugs i had no amunity to this sickness. Even today with all the help and there is a cure but i'am not in the area for this cure, so i just wait. I was told in the spring of 1992 that if i live right i could live up to 25 years that was if i lived right. I haven't done this not until i met Gordon so i don't know what life has instore for me or when my time is up. My husband has come with me to some of my appointment so he could understand this sickness plus he had to get the shots so he would not get this for himself it isn't fun somedays are ok other well there just aren't. If i could help just one person out there to understand drug are not the answer. As well as to the people that can see kids aren't alway able to open their mouths we need to watch and help them i know. It still happens out there and there isn't enough being done for the kids . There wasn't anyone helping me when i was one but things are different now we can speak up. I know in my case i look in the eyes of every child i walk by the reason being is it was done to me i can look into the eyes of someone that has been hurt in the same way as it was done to me all i can say is the eys tell it all the saddness, the lonelyness and the emptyness it is there just look.

MELODY BELIEVED ME

Melody and i had been friends for years. Our friendship didn't get off to a very good start, but we ended up being good friends and still are. Mel was the only friend that i could talk to and she believed me. Pastor R Mayon listened and had trusted in my words no body had ever listened not like they did. One night after her mother and father had been divorced her dad was with some other woman already by this time. I was over to stay a few days, he had been drinking lots not just on that day all of the time now. He was doing his drinking in the kitchen when he got up and came into Melodys' room he threw a few green bags onto the her bed where we sat. I asked her what was in the bags she told me pot i asked her what do we have to do with that stuff? she told me her dad gettings her to roll this stuff for him sometimes. We opened the bags and started rolling this stinky stuff it took a long time there was lots of it there. I had never seen that stuff in the past until then but she showed me how to roll it up. After some time i we heard him walk past Mel bedroom door. Mel and i finished doing what he asked of us so we carried it in to his room. He told melody to go feed the dog plus to do something else for him it would take her maybe ten minutes she said stay talk with dad i will be right back.

I sat on the edge of the bed to watch the tv he had in his room. I certainly never in a million years thought he would have done what he did that night. He grabbed me pulling me into his bed he had no underware on, he tried to kiss me and he also tried to take my pant down i knew what he was doing ,but i was going to let this happen. I pushed away from him a ran out the bedroom door and into Melodys' room slamming the door. Melody came to talk with me as i sat sobbing on her bed, she told me she would listen and i told her. As i told her i thought her would believe this and that night would be the end of our friendship, but it wasn't. The way her action was made me think that night made me think it had been done before. I can only hope and prey it wasn't done to her. She and i are still best friend today This is one person in my life that knows everything she lived with my mother before she pasted away, Melody is more a sister than my own sisters have ever been. I can say i think maybe it was because her and i being in the same youth group, confermation and scout maybe this is what made her and i so close. I believe it was a higher power that is how we met the rest is up to us.

NOW and THEN

I prey on a daily basis for my life to change for the better, but i still keep doing that praying and hoping for a life. I mean a real life, filled with love, trust, honestly. This seems to be too much that i 'am asking for, you get either one or the other. Never have i found the in one man not until now anyway. Back then life went now and time passed us by but we can't just give up on finding the things we want in our livesi would tell myself this a lot of time just so i wouldn't give up. If this weren't the case i would have given up years ago, believe me. My life has been one scary experience after the other. It seems as if i have been living in a horror show and not able to get out of the screen. I know it seems hard to believe that one person could go throught as much as i have. I will tell you this, not one thing that i have written here is a lie.

I'm not happy with all i have done to myself with out any help from others either. When i was hanging around with an ansavory group of people i did some stuff i don't want to face up to, but i think i should. Maybe this too may help me to see things in ways i never have. On winters night while my mom was still alive i went to my sons' fathers' place he lived just across the road and my mom was sleeping at the time. Plus i had a key to his place so off i went and as i opened the door he had a can to his mouth. He looked at me like a deer in the head lights, i asked him what he was doing? he told me it was called free bassing cocaine which meant cooking it and smoking it. He handed the can to me this was a big mistake i took it. This was a start of a nothing bad adventure for me. This went on for hours and then days, i would take off when my mom slept and smoke crack. It wasn't long after this when i took the break that the health nurses had told me to take. All the sudden i had something in my life that made me forget about everything at home and in the past. I didn't want to remember this that stuff not at that time anyway that why i did that stuff. I often blame myself for my mothers' pasting now too, because if i never walked across the road that night i would have never seen or tried that stuff. I think if i didn't go there that night none of what happened would have taken place. Then i would have never taken the over night break i took. Maybe my mom would have been with me fighting still instead of in the ground i think it was because she gave up because of being at Darleens place. It was because this garbage was so important to me at that time in my life, that my aunt was able to take my mom away, to live with her. This is one thing i just have not been able to forgive myself for not even today. I can't change anything now she is gone and that was then. Now i look at all that i have put my self through since my mother has pasted away. It seems to me looking back that once she had gone i went looking for something i don't know what i was looking for, but what i found was a lot of trouble along the way. Today things aren't as bad as they once were but i still don't live my life dreams i guess i'am asking to much. I want to be on the same land as my horses and own the land so i will always have my own home, i have said this in the past ,but most people have always had a home even when they were kids. I never have had this in my life time. It sure would be nice if this happened before i get to sick to enjoy any part of a so called good life what ever this may be. Maybe i have been living this good life and didn't know. Now today this have been better since i found Gordon i have said this before, but i was used to being with my horses for five years we lived with them when we rented a farm. That is the problem when you rent the owner can say at anytime "you have to move" for what ever reasons they may have. If we owned our own place i wouldn ever have to listen to those words again, i still can dream.

SHE IS GONE

Everyone i have spoken to since my mother has past tells me thing will get better, the pain will get easier to live with and live goes on. I say to people that say those words" maybe if you have had a normal life with a mother in it. With them knowing i have not had such a life. So while i have been waiting for these good things to start and for things to get better what have i done!I had one long term dysfunctional relationship which finally ended and i did end up with one good thing going out of this relationship which was my son. On the other hand his father Mitchell and i met only because of the drug life. I was going to leave him at one point until i found out i was with child. I wanted to give my son a chance to have a mother and father that stay together. This is exactly what i tried to do for twelve years. I would have stood for most things, but the cheeting and coming home with crabs i could put up with it. He didnt just do it once he was doing it over and over he would say he's going to work and sometimes he wouldn't be home with a pay cheque but he would bring home something. I had to start thinking about my son i did want him to have a mom and dad but not in a dysfunctional family life i had that with out the parent living in the same house i thought i would give him a chance. I left him many times and i took kim back until after my mother past away. The day my mom had past away he helped me along with a couple other by telling me here this will kill the pain that was cocaine. After i had been up for days i could stand still i wasn't eating and these people were used to using this drug i wasn't. Donna came and gave me another drug that would bring me down with out telling me if you do this one more than three time your body needs it. That was the most addictive drug i have have done. I went through years of steeling for it. I also went to jail so many times i was in more than i was out for six years. Once i got out of the Edmonton Prision for Wemen i have never been back to jail. I stay away from my sons' father and i 'am only with one man now. I met him before i went into the wemen prision. He stood beside me throughout everything. I had left big Mitchell and moved in with him about three or four month before going to jail. I met him while working for Mark was the only friend i had. He and his wife were very nice people mark had a son my sons' age they got along good too. Mark knew i was in trouble so he gave me a job a real job. He was a balif and would take me to drive cars for him. When he had a house to take away from someone he got me to pack the place up. Somedays i would work for ten hours a day. This help my money problems too. He tried to help me so i had to be honest he was a good friend and understood me so. When i told him i was using drugs with was where the money went to all of the time. It got to the point that Mitchell wouldn't go to work he went out to steel instead and i worked for mark. I would leave money at home so when i got home i would have my drugs waiting. Mitchell was taking my money and doing all the drugs up before i got homeat the end. This was when i started calling Gordon up more often and seeing him when he was in town because of his job as a trucker somedays he was out of town this is why i moved in with him. He was great plus he took very good care of me while i was living with him and when i was in jail too. He was good for and with my son he would play car and kid games stuff his own dad never did with him i never had anyone in my life like this man. I wasn't in love with him but i wanted him in my life. Because of the way he treated me, without sex being involved in our relationship. I didn't want to loose him so i told him about my past and what mt mother had done plus the foster stuff he said that he understood because he has four sisters only one brother, living with his sisters taught him about the woman and our problems.

I got out of jail and finished my porole in 2002 this was when we moved in together again. We have had our up and downs but he is a great man we were married on Novemeber 27, 2004. Now that my life is on track i wonder if i will ever be living my life dream which is to own a acerage with our own home on it. This way no one can say you have to move i sold the place or your kicked out again. I got myself two horses again in 2003. The last place we were renting these people decided one day they didn't want horses on their land only their own cows so again we were told we had to move. The funny thing is they knew we had the horses before we moved to their acerage. When we move in to their place it was the worse place i had ever seen but i would live anyway to be with my horses. I wanted the place and i told them i would fix the place up which i did while Gordy was at work i would work at make this place a home. I got it looking so good that the neighbour would come in and tell me how nice it looks anyway once these people came to get the rent money and saw how nice i had the place with rock gardens and all weed cut down plus i had wall papered and painted the inside and outside of the house they didn't care . I asked them to give us just a little room for the horses as it turns out i pay two hundred a month to keep my horses in the place where they are now. So in order to be living my dream i want to be living with my horses, on our own land. I have noticed even as a adult things aren't very easy, they don't get easier either. My husband works everyday and most times he gone at 4am and doesn't get home until 7 or 8pm. I would like to do things for him to show him how much i love him and to thank him for all he has done for me for the past 5 years.

BELIEVE ME

Why don't they believe us? Why would we lie about this sort of thing? kids don't lie. The way i grew up i thought it was right i thought everyone went though the same thing i was taught wrong. My mother let thing happen to me so many times it is hard to recall them all. Everytime i told her about what had happened to me i was told things like"you won't be believed, so don't say nothing, or if you say anything you will be sent away. The thing i was told most would be you must had led them on what ever that meant at the time i didn't know. I thought at first my mother could do something like this after all she is my mom right? i would say to myself but one day she had her friends son watch us kids as she went out drinking. He was the baby sitter from hell he was our care giver for the day but he was all but that. Once mom had gone he said to come to his moms'place to get ice cream cones but my hands were small so i ran down the hall with one in my hand at a time when it was the last cone that ment i got it. I ran down the hall thinking nothing but ice dream when i went in the apartment the door shut behind me it was all so fast, he was waiting for me. He drug me into his room tieing me to the posts of the bed. Once i was tied up he got all his clothing off and then cut mine of with a knife in the mean while he cut me as well. I t seemed to take forever before he finished doing what he wanted to me he wasn't finished, i think he was going to do it again. That was when i heard lauging coming from the outside door, sure eounghit was my mom and his mom. All i could think was my mom will save me at that time he cut two of the rope off of the bed but they were still on me, the other two i had cut with the knife he had left on the bed. Whe i got them off i ran into the closet calling my mom, crying out 'help me mom help me" What happened next was a shock to me my mother came in the room told me to get up and sent me home see me stand there with no clothing my cothing was on the floor cut up

yet still no help from my own mother. I did run home with rope burns on my arms leg and tears runnign down my face. Mom came home but, not long. Only long enough to tell me to not say anything again i hear her say this. After years ofthis i started thinking that i didn't like the feeling i had inside my heart. It was a sickening feeling. Most times i would run some place after it happened and cry. I didn't, nor do i understand how adult could watch this go on around them. It took until i was sixteen when i was living in my foster home, to be able to talk to someone about it again. The person just happened to be Pastor R Mayon,

he was my pastor he was the best human i have ever met. I still remember him ,and think about himand what he did for me. I was in a foster home for thirteen years in Tomahawk Alberta. There was only one person i told to other than him and her and i are still friend to this day Melody Z. Theday io finally opened up to my pastor i asked him 'when will this stuff stop ' he asked me what i was talking about, i thought that he would know what i was talking about after all he was a man, but he didn't. I didn't talk at first. I thought i was in trouble. This was what had been instilled in my head all my life but after awhile i did open up to him

once i started he couldn't beleieve his ears. He was the first person i had ever spoken with that listened to me. Hours pasted he just sat listening. He didn't interuppt me at all. I felt so safe while talking with him. I will never forget the feeling of all that burned lifting off my chest. Once i stopped talking i broke down. The feeling of finally being safe came over me, safe for naw anyway. He knew what was going on where i was living now, plus all that happened before the foster homes, so he got me out of there that day. I was able to stay with Melody for now she was my best friend then and still is today. That was the day i started thinking there are good people were out there. A few days later I was sent back to live with my mother in Edmonton. Things had not changed with her either i found out. The night i got into the City of Edmonton i ahd twenty one hunderd dollars on me i ask mom where can i put this until the bank opens she told me to put it in the flour jar it will be safe there she said. The trusting person i was i did what i was told to do. The next mornign i got up to go to the bank and i called for my mother, but she wan't around i got a bad feeling as i look at the flour jar, sure enough when i opened it and my money was gone. Once again i found out my mother hadn't changed at all. Afew days later once mom got home i asked about my money, she got mad right from the start telling me if i wanted to stay at her place i ahd to pay rent she wasn't back for one hour before this came out, but when i asked for my money. This was a different story she told me to get out she didn't touch my money i knew she differentit couldn't be no other way she was the only one who new the only one there. Once again i'am out of the house nothing new, i have always had to pay her one way or the other. Since being around my mom again i started thinking , all i had ever wanted in life was to have a real family, i had seen many of them while in forster care all of the people i met in Tomahawk had real families. From what i could see from the outside looking in to those families it seemed they had love in the family. I know tha everyone has family trouble but nothing like the family that i was raised in a dysfunctional family to say the least was what i lived in.

By the time i got old enough to understand things a little more i thought it was ok for a mother to sell her childern to men for money, after all i was told if i didn't do what i was told we wouldn't be able to eat. This crossed my mind a fews times when i got older because, while my mom would say 'if you don't do as your told how will your sisters and brother get to eat you will all go with out food today. I think back when i would be starving for not only effection but food as well. Although i did what was asked of me the food was no where to be found , i would open the fridge up to find it full of bottle not milk, or any thing us kids could have but boose. I do rememeber sitting beside the sink was beans and macaroni and cheese this was all we had ever eaten. Until i was four years old i had never seen or eaten a french fry and, i sure didn't get it from my mother either. For melself this has been a life long battle tring to deal with this and, there are many more of us out there some not knowing where to go so they turn to, in many cases i have seen girl turn to a female sex partener. Believe me i can understand this too because most have had the same life as i. The only thing i got out of my relationship was my son, his dad was no prise.

I was told many times in the past that i would after to do thing in life that i don't want to do everyone does but, if you just do it, we'll get it done and you will get to eat today. Plus your mother will be so pleased wit th you.

Once i had eoungh I found a male the i thought was the best person he had money looks a car everything i thoght i wanted in a man. Staying with him after awhile i just knew nothig was ever going to change things just were never going to be my dream life not while being with him anyway was mostly a waist of time. I only got one thing out of this relationship and this was my baby boy. I tryied so hard to make it work, but the drugs got in the way he just made the wrong choice be picked the the live of drugs and robbery instead of his son and i. Where there was more to life i knew this, i just didn't know how to go about obtaining it. I had looked for it for so many years. So far in life in had nothing to show. I gave everything i had to my mother after getting out of foster care thinking that she would love me, if i did this for her.This wasn't true .I had met a very good man one that never pushed sex on me not once time, This was very different he started out being all i could even ask but, still i wonder can he be for real? is today the day he changes the rules? on it often,. i didn't do it to trun other men on it did it for my own reason , health. plus inot feeling great but i want nothing more than to have a acerage for kid to come riding iam a horses , i would teach them. My dream is and has been for me to get a farm where i an have way word kids to my home make them feel trusted, love and hel[p them when they ask for for. Most adult say came back later or sorry can help, or we are closed down, caqll the kids help line. Honestlt when kids need help they need it know. I my dream comes true i will sell lots of book and sell them for the land i need so i can take in younger kids male, female ned different than the male do just just don't take the time to understand.

I can prey, hope for chances, for a better life. Iam going to tell you something that iam not so happy about, i was into the drug life for sometime and this wasn't all i did for my drug habit either for a very short time i was selling myself thinking i was hurting those men but this wasn't the cares i made myself feel wrose than when i started. In the begining i thoght i was hurting the men, as they had hurt me in the past. I have often thought about how a person could go throught even half as i and still have love my heart for man kind. Mainly the love i carry in my heart is for the children. Today i can look into the eyes of a child and see the same pain as i had in my life but it show in the eyes of the youngters, One day i fill my dreams which includ have the kids that have been abused or foster kids, will stay on my acerage in the country.

Where there are no adults only kids, horses and alot of fun for all.

IT'S NOT ANY EASIER

It got easier with everytime it was done to me. Mom told me to just get over it, with and then i wouldn't have to do it again. I believed her each time she said to me this will be the last time , but the last time never did come. She would say look up at the ceiling like i told you before it will get easier, getting your mind off what's happening to me was one thing but the pain was another how to you get this off your mind, i asked her a couple times, she would just say don't be a baby, be a big girl for your mommy. I could never get used to it no matter what i did tring to trick my mind, in fact now i hate sex. What was done to me as i child made my sex life a whole bunch different than what it should be i'm sure of thisI would love to not be so scared to take my man hand or take a walk into the sunset as it starts to get dark. I would like to be able to do even the smallest of things like take a show with the door opened or showering with my husband. There is much more that i would like to do but, i'am just to scared still today. Night time is the scarest part of the day, i have been working on it and it is getting easier for me but, each night when i go to bed i think of an excuse just incase he wants sex. Even when i do have sex with my husband, it is sad to think this way but, sometimes it is as if i put myself back into my childhood and stair at the wall until it is over. This isn't the way i want to be, it is just the way it is sometimes. There has been nights when i would be in the same bed as him but as soon as he would reach out to hug me or touch me i would hit him and move away or run away. Even in the day time i have done the samething. One day i was washing the dishes when he came up from behind me without saying anything as he came towards me, as soon as he reached out i had a feeling i truned around so fast and hit him breaking his glasses in his face. I have asked him in the past not to do things like that, i have told him everything about my past and what my mother used to do to me. I guess he did think it was as bad as it really is he does know now but, there are time he forgets.

Mostly i'm very lucky to have him as a husband he is very understanding, sometimes i wonder for just how long he will be this way. I'm sure we have all seen when two people think they are getting something in their mate, and after a few months or a year, it all changes. I my case i have not changed although i try to in a good way. I have talked with many different doctors in the past. The first time was in 1979 i hated it firstly because he was a male second he didn't think a person could go through what i went through and not in crazy in the head he told me this. I wanted help so i didn't give up besides i was told keep looking and eventually i would find the right one for me. I never found that person back then. I found more males that i just didn't care for nor did i trust any of them. They all said the same thing if i endured all i said i would be crazy. I'am one person that has tried to learned from my past not get angry. Anyway when i did let myself think to hard on the past i tried to kill myself at least five times. Not once did it work out for me i'am still here. That when i started to think maybe someone up there has a bigger plan for me. So here i'am waiting on the day for the good things start to come my way. So far i found Gordon my husband who knows, maybe someday i will be living my dream life. I preyed to God for someone to come into my life that i would be able to talk with and trust in. Just when i started to write about the past i did find the lady, i will never forget her she did treat me as i have been used to in the past, and one day i took my book into her so i wouldn't have to talk as much she could read it and then we could start off my her knowing why i need her. On the third visit with her she was the one crying she believed me and didn't do as the male did. I went back to see her for around two years and just like i told her in the begining when we first met, everytime i grow to like someone trust in them and pour my heart out they either die or move away i was right. It was a good thing for her she found a better job but, for me again i lost someone i trusted. I don't think i can go through this again starting over is just to hard.